PIANO · VOCAL · GUITAR

TOBY KEITH
SHOCK'N Y'ALL

ISBN 0-634-07425-3

HAL·LEONARD®
CORPORATION
7777 W. BLUEMOUND RD. P.O. BOX 13819 MILWAUKEE, WI 53213

Visit Hal Leonard Online at
www.halleonard.com

I LOVE THIS BAR

Words and Music by TOBY KEITH
and SCOTTY EMERICK

WHISKEY GIRL

Words and Music by TOBY KEITH
and SCOTTY EMERICK

Original key: G♭ major. This edition has been transposed up one half-step to be more playable.

AMERICAN SOLDIER

Words and Music by TOBY KEITH
and CHUCK CANNON

In a steady four

I'm just try'n' to be a fa-ther, raise a daugh-ter and a son._ Be a
do it for the mon-ey, there's _ bills that I ___ can't pay._ I don't

lov-er to ___ their moth-er, ev-'ry-thing to ev-'ry-one. ___ Up and
do it for ___ the glo-ry, I just do it an-y-way. ___ Pro-

at 'em bright _ and ear-ly, I'm all bus-'ness in ___ my suit. Yeah, I'm
vid-ing for ___ our fu-ture's, my re-spon-si-bil-i-ty. ___ Yeah, I'm

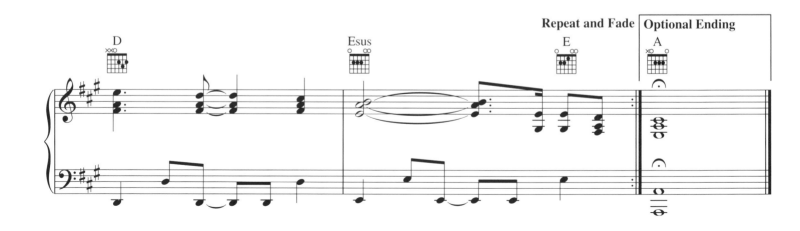

IF I WAS JESUS

Words and Music by CHUCK CANNON
and PHIL MADEIRA

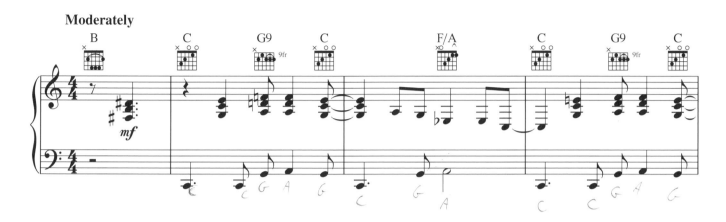

If I was Je - sus,   I'd have some real long_____
- sus,   I'd have some friends that were poor._
- sus,   I'd come back from the dead_

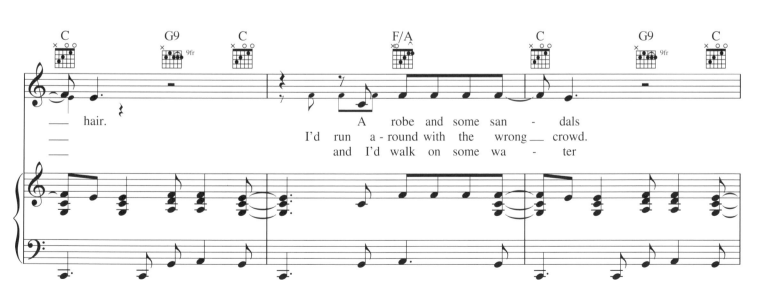

_____ hair.
_____ A robe and some san - dals
_____ I'd run a - round with the wrong_ crowd.
_____ and I'd walk on some wa - ter

TIME FOR ME TO RIDE

Words and Music by TOBY KEITH
and CHUCK CANNON

I be-lieve it's time for me to ride.

Repeat and Fade

Optional Ending

SWEET

Words and Music by TOBY KEITH,
SCOTTY EMERICK and CHUCK CANNON

DON'T LEAVE, I THINK I LOVE YOU

Words and Music by TOBY KEITH
and RONNIE DUNN

Don't _ leave, _____ I think I love _ you. _

I just saw the rest of my life. Hon-ey, you're in it. Won't you

hear what I say? _ Give me just a min-ute. Don't _ leave, _____

I know you think I'm cra - zy and you prob-a -bly should. I would-n't

make this up. I could-n't dream this good.

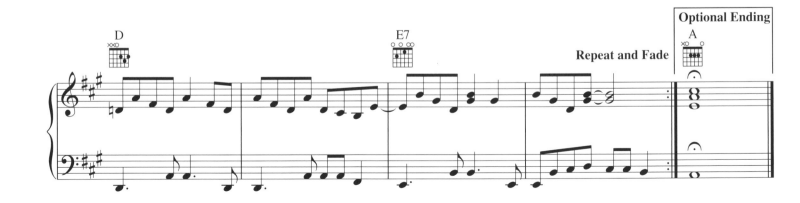

Optional Ending

Repeat and Fade

NIGHTS I CAN'T REMEMBER, FRIENDS I'LL NEVER FORGET

Words and Music by TOBY KEITH
and SCOTTY EMERICK

Me and J B and Son - ny, we grew up ___ on the bud - dy plan.
___ one sum - mer night at a par - ty, we were soph - 'mores hang - in' out by the lake.

Weren't we some bad moth - ers, ___ clos - er than broth - ers, had a
I got off ___ on some wine with a wait - ress, Son - ny had a girl -

BADDEST BOOTS

Words and Music by
TOBY KEITH

THE CRITIC

Words and Music by
TOBY KEITH